Humbled

by

His Presence

Meeting YHWH at the Threshing Floor

Huldah Dauid

Dedication

This book is dedicated to Yahuah. The FIRST and the BEST of everything belongs to Him. I am humbled by the opportunity to be a vessel for His Kingdom. I thank Him for being my portion and my refuge.

Acknowledgements

I also want to thank my family and companions on this walk for always encouraging me. I want to thank every woman that poured into me at the most pivotal parts of life. I want to give special thanks to: My Mom, My Magmom (Karma D.), Aunt Monae, Granny (Sheila), Grandma Gloria, Auntie Lorie, Joslyn, Armelia, Janelle, Dezarae, Jasmine, Auntie CoCo, Aunt Emma, Latrice, Michelle, Patricia Luckett, and last, but not at all in the least, the women in the TBFC Congregation. Without all of them I would not be a fraction of the woman I am today. I want to thank my girls, Jade and Arielle for their sacrifice, although they are probably too young to realize what I am doing. I appreciate them for always being my reason to never give up. I want to thank my Dad for staying on my case about getting things done. For meeting me whenever I needed a pep talk, and for always putting things into perspective. And finally to my Husband, thank you for putting up with me. You, my friend, are a saint! Thank you for being my sounding board, my Adon, my sparing partner, and my best friend. אניאוהבתאותך (I Love You). I mean that Concretely, not Abstract!

Preface

This book is a compilation of personal meditation and devotionals that are written from my quiet time with Yah (God). As a wife and mother, I have been searching for a deeper relationship with my Heavenly Father. In Seeking my understanding of Him has been expanded through a willingness to be challenged in the studying of His Word. In my old understanding I sought to "arrive," but now I know I am on a wonderful journey, and like any journey it is best taken with a companion. A companion is someone who is traveling in the same direction as you are. My reason for writing, sharing, and encouraging is to show that we are on the same path of righteousness, ultimately leads to the Father's House. All of us who are seeking a deeper relationship are going through similar changes, and through this process my goal is to be transparent, to let you know that I am right here with you as a companion. I've attempted to allow a glimpse into my life through some of the studies that have personal significance, as well as into my heart. What is often seen on the outside of a person's life is only a fraction of who they really are. In this devotional the goal is to remove the hard outer shell from the heart, and to submit to transformation. Humbled in His Presence was primarily written for you as an aid in receiving shalom during this spiritual journey of deeper understanding.

Introduction

As you journey through this devotional, the goal is to challenge you. I know many of us hate a challenge, especially when it comes to our faith. We believe that if anything should be simple, it should be our walk as believers. Though I wish I could confirm this type of thinking, I cannot, because transformation takes a challenge.

This devotional purposely uses words that you may not be familiar with, and will use the light of "The Word" to illuminate places you may not have even known were dark. All I ask is that through these 21 days you are patient. I recommend that you purchase a journal and document your thoughts and feelings about the topics and lessons that are shared. Be honest with yourself, and more importantly with your Heavenly Father.

In your journal, write what you think about the title and the verse before you read it, then after reading, express what has changed about your initial thought. Seeing the transformation of the Word on paper often yields much better results, allows you to later reflect on where you were, and also where you would like to be. While going through this devotional, schedule time for you and your Elohim (Most High) alone. Try to stay on track, then use the end of the week to reflect on what you wrote in your journal throughout the week. Taking some intimate time with God (Yah) will allow you to work out complicated questions that may arise during meditation on the concepts that will be presented.

In the next couple of paragraphs I am going to define some terms that are used in the devotion, and some names that you may not be familiar with. This is purposely done to challenge you to dig deeper into the word. Please feel free to contact me if you have any questions about new or unfamiliar information you encounter.

Biblical Translations

A Bible translation is just that, a translation. Most Bibles we have in our homes are a translation. They are, more often than not, a good faith attempt by an individual to give you a better understanding of scripture in your native tongue, but in reality they are just that, an attempt. The only way to really understand what is said in scripture is to see it through the culture of the original Hebrew writers.

While many of us, who are trying to learn the Hebrew language, would like to tell you that translations don't have bias, that would not be the truth. The truth is that we all have bias and our experiences and culture often become a driving force in our understanding. The same is true for many translators; their denomination, culture, and theological bias are evident in their translations and commentaries. With that being said, the only way to really rid ourselves of these biases is to understand the culture and context of the original writers, and then filter our understanding through their mindset. This is not only necessary for the "Old Testament," but also the "New." Although the copies of the "New Testament" we have are in Greek, it is overwhelmingly evident that the writers were thinking with a Hebrew mind. It was a long commonly held misconception that the New testament was only written in "slang" or colloquial Greek, known as Koine

Greek. This was thought to be used to speak to the common people, but what has now become evident through deeper study is that the "New Testament Greek" was written with a Hebrew mindset and culture, using Greek words. What was thought to be the "slang" Greek, was in fact, perfect Hebrew thought that gives clues to get back to the actual Hebrew and the cultural context.

**If you want to look further you can look up the findings of clues for Hebrew copies of the New Testament, and their former existence before the diaspora. Also search out the Gospel to the Hebrews (different from the book of Hebrews in our canonized Bible).

Abstract versus Concrete

In Western culture we are always changing. We add new words to our dictionary as they are birthed out of pop culture and evolving linguistics. We are the best at determining what something means to us. We use our personal definition as the premise for an argument with those around us about their different interpretation. We are the poster children for "agree to disagree."

While we may want to interject personal feelings into the interpretation of scripture, biblically we are forbidden to do so. The scripture must be interpreted by scripture, and then by the meaning of each word in context.

In scripture words mean things, and it is the Word that does not change. People change, times change, but because the Word is tied to the existence of heaven and earth, it cannot.

> For verily I say unto you, Till heaven and earth pass, one jot or one tittle shall in no wise pass from the law, till all be fulfilled.
>
> Matthew 5:18

The Word of Yah is concrete. All of the words in the Bible go back to something that can be seen, touched, tasted, smelled, or heard. When discovering the truth of the Word, Yah would have us to rely on our observation rather than our own interpretation. He defines His Word with His Word, and this interpretation is not based upon how we feel or what we have personally experienced. From the beginning, His Word has been the standard, and that remains true today.

As you go through this devotional you will be given concrete meaning of words like "love," "repent," and "keep," among many others. In this 21 day period, the challenge will be to remove your old ideas and search out the original intent. A proper understanding will allow you to worship and walk as a believer without guessing. The goal is to remove opinion and man-made influences so that the Word of Yah is the final say in all things.

Culture and Context

Everything you read in scripture is connected to cultural references. It is the understanding of these cultural references that allow us to keep the Word in proper context. When the words of the writers are interpreted abstractly and applied outside of their original culture we run the risk of losing, or dramatically watering down the original intent of scripture. The Bible is full of idioms and sayings that are only known in the context of that time period. While it is easier to just find out what a word would mean to you personally, doing extra study and research would take you to the root of the true meaning and reveal the hidden jewels of the Word. In these studies regular life issues are taken and applied in a way that anyone can understand while still preserving the original context of the Biblical authors and their culture. Because Yah (God) doesn't change, I am passionate about giving you a timeless understanding of His truth that is palatable, even for those who are not familiar with the Hebrew culture.

Yahoshua/ Yeshua

Contrary to popular belief "Jesus" was not the name that the Angel told Mariam (Hebrew for Mary) to name our Messiah. There are several reasons why that would not have been possible. First, because there is no letter J in the Hebrew language. Also because names mean something in the Hebrew language. The Messiah would come, not only in the person of, but also in the name of the living El (God). The Angel said that his name would be called "Jesus, because He would save His people from their sins."

> And she shall bring forth a son, and thou shalt call
> His name Yahoshua: for He shall save His people
> from their sins.
>
> Matthew 1:21

That name is Yahoshua, Hebrew for "Yah is Salvation." In the Old Testament when you see the word "salvation," if you have the time to look up the name "Jesus", you will see the name of Yeshua/ Yehoshua/ Yahusha even Joshua, but never Jesus. Pretty cool, right?

It is my personal conviction based on my study and my understanding of proper names that no matter where in time or on the planet a person travels, that their name should remain the same. I have an even stronger conviction about the name of my Messiah. If there is no name (character) under heaven or earth by which we must be saved, I believe that it is my personal duty to know His name.

> And there is salvation in no one else, for there is no other name under heaven that is given among people by which we must be saved.
>
> Acts 4:12

Because English is my first language I understand that it may be difficult to adjust to names outside of your native tongue, but I personally try very hard to learn people's names as they were given. The same is true for our Messiah. He was given a name and although it may be hard adjusting to a different name, it's out of respect that we call Him what He (was/is) intended to be called. My inability to bend outside of my comfort zone does not give me the right to change the King of Kings and Master of Masters name to suit me. Unless I encounter scriptural evidence that we are able to change His name I will be using the proper name of the Messiah or the Hebrew shortened form Yeshua.

Yah/Yahuah/Abba

Because I already covered my convictions for names I will be brief in this section. Psalm 68:4 gives us the shortened form of God's proper name.

> Sing to God, sing praises to his name. Lift up a song to the rider on the clouds—his name is Yah—and rejoice before him.
>
> Psalm 68:4 (LEB)

> Sing unto God, sing praises to his name: extol him that rideth upon the heavens by his name Jah, and rejoice before him.
>
> Psalm 68:4 (KJV)

> Sing ye to God -- praise His name, Raise up a highway for Him who is riding in deserts, In Jah [is] His name, and exult before Him.
>
> Psalm 68:4 (YLT)

> Sing to God! Sing praises to his name! Extol him who rides on the clouds: to Yah, his name! Rejoice before him!
>
> Psalm 68:4 (WEB)

The long form can be found beneath the title LORD. If you own a lexicon have Google, look up the proper name of God. While God has many titles, He only has one Name. His name expresses all of His attributes. His Name means, "I AM THAT I AM," or "I WILL BE WHO I WILL BE."

> And God said unto Moses, I Am That I Am: and He said, Thus shalt thou say unto the children of Israel, I Am hath

sent me unto you. And God said moreover unto Moses, Thus shalt thou say unto the children of Israel, Yahuah God of your fathers, the God of Abraham, the God of Isaac, and the God of Jacob, hath sent me unto you: this is my name for ever, and this is my memorial unto all generations.

Exodus 3:14-15

This name is found in the names of the prophets, like Jeremiah (YerimiYah or YerimiYahu). His name is made up of four consonants יהוה' (Yod, Hey, Vav/Waw/Uau, Hey). While it is common in religious commentaries and circles that there are no vowels in Hebrew, those of us who have studied the language know that the consonants also serve as vowels. His name has not been lost, it has been removed from our mouths because we were told not to use it. While I won't get into the argument of pronunciation, I will say that the use of the Name Yah/Yahuah/Yahweh (or any commonly used variation) will be the way that I will address the Father (Abba) in this devotional.

**If you would like further study or a list of over 100 times that Yah tells us to use HIS name I will gladly email them to you.

Don't be intimidated by Hebrew Words

In the bibliography I have provided resources that will allow you to dig deeper and gain more understanding. Also I have done my best to keep the actual Hebrew words to a minimum and focus more on what they mean. It's never too late to learn or experience something new. I have faith in you, and remember I am also available as a tool through this journey.

DAY: ONE

Incline Your Ear

And after the earthquake a fire; but YHWH was not in the fire: and after the fire a still small voice.
1 Kings 19:12

Today is the day to be still. Every day we get so caught up in the mundane and menial confines of our own existence that we miss many of the more important things in life. The hustle and bustle of the rat race is so loud that at times we have trouble even hearing ourselves think. We say to those around us, "some quiet time would be much appreciated," but the necessity of our presence drowns out such a pure plea.

Silence is often the most under prescribed remedy to an over stimulated mind. Most often on our spiritual journey, we fail to take out time to be silent. We are always looking for the loud thunder of YHWH's voice, and forget that when He wants our attention, He doesn't always raise His voice, but sometimes He beckons us with a gentle whisper.

I became acquainted with one of the most beautiful souls about 13 years ago. She is an older woman, and she is of the most regal kind. Her steps light, her words few, but a powerful presence. With all of her confidence, the thing that stood out the most were her soft words. At first, I didn't understand how her gentle disposition was so captivating. Talking to her always required getting very close to hear what she was saying. It wasn't until I got older that I realized something very significant about her that carried over into my spiritual life, and often ministers to me. It was almost like the a-ha! moment. She was not acting by happenstance, but she moved and spoke that way on purpose.

When a person speaks softly, you must get close enough to hear. This close proximity shows your attentiveness to what is being said, it also means that they care enough to speak to you. They allow you into their personal space where there is intimate communication, often meant only for your ears. The same is true with Yah. He often allows His voice to become lower while others seem louder, so that we turn everyone else down, and everything around us off to find His whisper. Taking time to incline our ear, rather than get frustrated shows that we want to hear what He is saying, and it also means He has something important to say to us. Today, as the voice of Yah seems far away or small, incline your ears to the word that He has just for you.

Scripture Reading:

My son, if thou wilt receive my words, and hide my commandments with thee; So that thou incline thine ear unto wisdom, and apply thine heart to understanding; Yea, if thou criest after knowledge, and liftest up thy voice for understanding; If thou seekest her as silver, and searchest for her as for hid treasures; Then shalt thou understand the fear of Yahuah, and find the knowledge of God.

Proverbs 2:1-5 (KJV)

"My sheep hear My voice, and I know them, and they follow Me; and I give eternal life to them, and they will never perish; and no one will snatch them out of My hand."

John 10:27-28 (KJV)

DAY: TWO

True Love

So if you faithfully obey the commands I am giving you today, to love YHWH your Elohim and to serve him with all your heart and with all your soul, then I will send rain on your land in its season.

Deuteronomy 11:13-14

We have all experienced that awkward moment where emotions meet verbal expression. The words sit in the back of your throat like a weight. You twiddle with your thumbs and look down shyly. You get that goofy feeling in your stomach, and almost like a bad bout with food poisoning, it comes up almost unannounced...I LOVE YOU! We reach for our lips almost as if we wished to be able to grab back the expression of ultimate devotion. The vulnerability and awkwardness is almost too much to bear as we wait for the response of the receiving party. For many of us, this exchange is more than familiar.

In the English language, saying "I love you" is the highest form of emotional expression, but in reality it is about context. A guy telling his friend , "I love you, man", after a drunken episode is not the same as him telling his significant other that he loves her. Likewise, a woman expressing how much she LOVES those shoes, is not the same as pouring out her heart in adoration for the man that makes her heart skip a beat (although the shoes might be a close second). Nonetheless, in English, we are given the ability to change the definition of the word "love" based upon the context that it is used. In the Hebrew language, we are not given this type of luxury. In Hebrew, words mean something, and they are expressed concretely. The word "love" is no longer a misnomer for failure to use word precision. Once placed into the Hebrew, we get a true understanding of just what love is, and how it is to be expressed and reciprocated. Once we understand love, we have a better understanding of how God loves us, and how we are to reciprocate that love back to Him, as well as to one another.

The Hebrew word for love is AHAVAH (אהבה). When broken all the way down to its base root, this means "to give," and more accurately "I give," which also means love. To love someone means to give. While this may sound very elementary, there is more to be gleaned. In Western Christian religion, we have been convinced that the God of the Old Testament, and all that He "gave" is no longer of any affect, because He ultimately gave His only begotten son, thus, nullifying any former act of giving. When love is defined as giving, then all that the Most High gave was out of His love. If we survey creation to the giving of the law, we see a God who loves His creation very deeply. This love can be similarly seen in the giving of a mother to her child.

When a woman becomes pregnant, she immediately begins giving. Her womb and her body are no longer hers, and every-thing she does is for the sake of the child (we will cover the womb later in our devotional). The same is so with our Abba. Before the foundation of the word, He had us in mind. Not just humanity, but you and I. He put the plan of salvation in everything around us in order to draw us back to Him. When we get to Moses at Sinai, we get a culmination of His expressed love for us as a people. He gives us a guide to love Him back. It is one thing to be given love, almost in the form of a secret admirer. You receive all this love, and once you are completely enamored with this person, there is a burn to know who He is. It is at Mount Sinai that our Elohim Himself. He gives us His name and He shows us how to love Him. This is the most beautiful picture of a love that gives. Yah has given us His heart (Torah) without reservation, and all He asks is that we heed to how He wants His love to be reciprocated. He wants us to do the best we can not to earn His love, because He gave it freely without us asking; but to be just as faithful as He was in sustaining us, even when we were yet sinners. In parallel, we are to show this same amount of love and devotion to our loved ones. We are to give our love with devotion to our spouse and our children, following in the footsteps of Sarah and heeding the will of the Most High without fear; but with great anticipation of what the fruit of our love, obedience, and discipline will yield if we are faithful to the call of loving, and giving with our whole hearts. God has put himself out there first, and is only waiting for our response to do all that He has said and commanded (Exodus 24:3).

Scriptural Reading:

> Give to every man that asketh of thee; and of him that taketh away thy goods ask them not again. And as ye would that men should do to you, do ye also to them likewise. For if ye love them which love you, what thank have ye? for sinners also love those that love them.

> Luke 6:30-33 (KJV)

You shall not seek vengeance, and you shall not harbor a grudge against your fellow citizens; and you shall love your neighbor like yourself; I am Yahweh.

Leviticus 19:18 (LEB)

And the second is like, namely this, Thou shalt love thy neighbor as thyself. There is none other commandment greater than these. And the scribe said unto him, Well, Master, thou hast said the truth: for there is one God; and there is none other but he: And to love him with all the heart, and with all the understanding, and with all the soul, and with all the strength, and to love his neighbour as himself, is more than all whole burnt offerings and sacrifices. And when Yeshua saw that He answered discreetly, He said unto him, Thou art not far from the Kingdom of God. And no man after that durst ask him any question.

Mark 12:31-34 (KJV)

For God so loved the world, that He gave his only begotten Son, that whosoever believeth in him should not perish, but have everlasting life.

John 3:16 (KJV)

DAY: THREE

Immersion

And YHWH called the dry ground "earth," and He called the collection of the waters "seas." And YHWH saw that it was good. And YHWH said, "Let the earth produce green plants that will bear seed—fruit trees bearing fruit in which there is seed—according to its kind, on the earth." And it was so.

Genesis 1:10-11

I grew up in a Baptist church. My grandmother was a very religious woman. One of her prayers for her grandchildren was that we would all be baptized by the age of 5. While her prayer was noble to say the least, her idea of baptism, and what it meant was not rooted in anything that I now understand as an adult. Needless to say, whether it was from her earnest prayer, or just the repetition of her plea, all of us were baptized.

There is not much I remember about the first five years of my life, but there is one thing that I cannot shake: THAT BAPTISM. At the time, I attended a fairly large church. The baptismal pool was in the front of the church building behind the pulpit. After my grandmother's, uhh, I mean my request for baptism, I was scheduled to be baptized on the first Sunday. My grandfather and another man whom I can't recall, were going to baptize me. I got all dressed up in white, including a white swimmers cap, because God forbid a "black" girl gets her hair wet, and was sent down the steps to the pool. As I stepped in the water, the only thing I could think about was water going up my nose. If that happened, surely I was going to DIE! When they got ready to baptize me, I had one hand on my grandpa's wrist and the other pinching my nose. They took me under. After what felt like 20 years, they brought me back up. That is all I remembered of my baptism experience, and it wouldn't be for another 20 years, when I was immersed in the way of my Hebrew ancestors, that I would understand why or what baptism was all about.

Some of the things I deduced as a freaked out 5-year-old were true. The first is they were really trying to kill me! Well not literally (hopefully), but the idea of baptism is associated with death. Not death of separation from Yah, but a death in order to be gathered into His Family. Let me explain. In Genesis 1:10-11, we see an easily overlooked picture of immersion:

> And God called the dry ground "earth," and He called the collection of the waters "seas." And God saw that it was good. And God said, "Let the earth produce green plants that will bear seed—fruit trees bearing fruit in which there is seed—according to its kind, on the earth." And it was so.

While I am quite sure that my grandmother was only being the best grandmother she could be, and not a theologian, her prayer has some biblical significance. The first immersion takes place in the beginning, and we get a working definition of what this immersion or baptism really means. In the Hebrew language, tevialh is the word for immersion. This word is also related to two other words, Mikveh (the location of immersion) and Qavah (to gather). These words together carry the meaning of being dipped in a particular location for the ultimate goal of gathering.

In Western culture, more specifically Western religion, practices have become embedded within ordinances that are often rooted in scripture, but have no real concrete idea of the meaning of these "traditions." Baptism falls into that category. As a child growing up in church, we are taught that baptism is a sign of obedience, and is not for salvation, and we are doing our job to be good followers of Messiah. While this is true, it is only a partial truth. We are actually being gathered into a family where we can be taught and then bear fruit. We see this point made by Messiah Yahoshua (Jesus) in his great commission.

> Therefore, go and make disciples of all the nations, baptizing them in the name of the Father and of the Son and of the Holy Spirit, teaching them to observe everything I have commanded you.

> Matthew 28:19-20 (KJV)

After the resurrection, we are baptized into the blood of the finished work of Messiah. Similar to the Passover, just as we died with Christ, now we also live in him, and are now given the opportunity to be obedient. And this obedience is how we bear fruit. Once the waters of our immersion are removed, the ground of our heart compelled us into the act of obedience should now show fruit of our transformation, from death in sins and trespasses to a new life of obedience. This new life comes with a new family, and a renewed covenant of obedience to our Most High, who from the foundation of the world showed us this ordinance that is important to the bringing forth of fruit.

Scripture Reading:

Buried with him in baptism, wherein also ye are risen with him through the faith of the operation of God, who hath raised him from the dead.

Colossians 2:12 (KJV)

John answered, saying unto them all, I indeed baptize you with water; but one mightier than I cometh, the latchet of whose shoes I am not worthy to unloose: He shall baptize you with the Holy Ghost and with fire:

Luke 3:16 (KJV)

DAY: FOUR

Broken Hearts

Yahuah is near to those who are heartbroken
and saves those who are crushed in spirit.
Psalm 34:18

It's only when a heart is shattered into pieces that Yah wants it. When we see broken things, we rarely see value in them. We don't thrift for a broken find. We want what is whole. The exact opposite is true of YHWH. A whole heart is a proud heart, and it shows no need of Him.

I know too often from personal experience and observation that no one calls on YHWH until they are in trouble, or in despair. It is not until there is no other way many of us, even believers, ever consult our Abba. But the truth of the matter is that's just how He likes it. When we come to Him broken, we have exhausted all other options, and are finally ready to place ourselves into His delicate hands.

It is the shattered pieces He uses to make His masterpiece. He is such a master artist that even with marred clay, at His potter's wheel, can He make a vessel for choice use. Whether it is a shattered marriage, a shattered opportunity, or shattered trust; in His Word is where we humbly place those pieces before Him. He can take our broken heart, and not just mend it, but make it better than before. Today, if you have broken pieces of your life that you are holding on to, trust that in the hands of Yah, they can be used in His service.

31

Scripture Reading:

For what nation is there so great, who hath God so nigh unto them, as Yahuah our God is in all things that we call upon him for?

Deuteronomy 4:7 (KJV)

The sacrifices of God are a broken spirit: a broken and a contrite heart, O God, you will not despise.

Psalm 51:17 (KJV)

Thou art near, O YHWH; and all thy commandments are truth.

Psalm 119:151 (KJV)

He healeth the broken in heart, and bindeth up their wounds.

Psalm 147:3 (KJV)

DAY: FIVE

My Hidden Faults

Who can perceive his errors? Acquit me from hidden faults.
Psalm 19:12

Most of us spend our whole lives hiding from everyone around us. We put on masks, smiles, or frowns as guards to conceal what is really going on inside. We have become the masters of disguise. Not wanting onlookers to evaluate us for who we really are. We are constantly putting up facades to reinvent ourselves, when in all reality we are never really allowing ourselves to be who Yah intended us to be. It is the real us Yah has chosen to minister and to witness to those around us. We are so busy fixing the outer image that the real us is dying, and we are neglecting to deal with the hidden woman. We never stop to think that in all of our concealing we are actually sinning against the Most High. We cover to the point that we don't even know who we are. It is not until we are exposed to the light of truth that we can even begin to let our guard down and truly be evaluated by Yah. You might say you live a "holy" life, but it's merely based on what a person doesn't know about you, and not on how you have actually lived. Let's take some time to think about the things that we do that we may not even know of? What about the things that others can't perceive? The things about us that loom in areas that only Yah can see? You know, those justified and unknown areas we conceal even from ourselves?

Many of us never stop to think there may be deeper meaning behind our errors. The corruption at the root of a problem can begin festering and rotting without us even knowing. These are things that we wouldn't want people to know. The things in our inner parts that make us cower in fear. If these things are exposed, will my husband still love me? Will my friends still like me? Will those who depend on me be let down? These are insecurities that Yah can be trusted with. He wants these fears, because not only is He the only one that can take away the fear, but He is the only One who can see who we really are and what we are hiding behind. While we cover our eyes not wanting to see the hurt or the gaping wound of our suppressed iniquities and transgressions, He is not shocked; because like a good Father, He already knew. Yah is not judging to tell someone else or to expose you. He is not looking to get ammunition or to say "I told you so." He is looking to heal. He is pulling away the bandage to find the gaping wound, and as the great physician, He is coming to repair and find the wrongs and make them right.

So often we share our errors with our friends and we are left feeling empty and unresolved, because we couldn't really open up like we wanted to. Yah is a friend who is closer than a brother and He cannot only look at the problem, but He is willing to change the circumstance. Allow Him to examine you. Let Him see the scars. Let Him see the pain. Because it is only when we are willing to let him in that He can shine light in the darkest places and bring life. The adversary seeks out that which is hidden in order to cause guilt. When we stop hiding, we become free and yes we have faults, but our faults are no longer instruments for blackmail by the accuser, but they are testimonies toward righteousness.

Scripture Reading:

Psalm 40

DAY: SIX

Emotions into Subjection

He that is slow to anger is better than the mighty; and He that ruleth his spirit than He that taketh a city.
Proverbs 16:32

I am sure I am not the only one who allows my emotions to get the best of me. Do you ever have those days where you wake up an emotional wreck, and then you drag your emotional wreck of a self onto an emotional rollercoaster? Well I am even a bit more radical, because I often drag my husband on that emotional rollercoaster with me.

Many of our emotions stem from issues we have masked, and not dealt with properly. So many times we clean up the house of our mind and heart from things that happened in the past, only to store them in a closet in our brain to be used at a later date. We say we forgive, and we even claim to have forgotten, but all the while we are hiding a little list of offenses in our back pocket to be used as ammunition for the next available moment. If I am not alone, can we take a moment of silence for all the loaded guns of hurt we carry? Because today we are going to put the safety on and remove the bullets.

I know better than most that stored emotions and pain profit nothing. As a frequent journal writer, and a very sensitive individual, I have found that I compartmentalize my hurt. When I do this, it leaves portals for new offenses to awaken old ones. This level of dysfunction is not healthy. It took a serious purge, fast, and much prayer for me to even consider letting go, because our emotions

37

and our hurt start to define who we are, and when we let them go, we feel as though we are losing a part of ourselves. Change doesn't only hurt when it's in the negative, even change for a good reason causes considerable amounts of discomfort. Although it's difficult today, we are putting our emotions in subjection. Our emotions and hurts cannot control or define who we are. When anything has more power than Yah does over us, it is in control. Our hurts and pains that create these emotions are idols of importance. Today we are tearing down idols and portals we have allowed to ruin relationships, causing us to be depressed, and to not live life to the fullest. Our emotions are not in subjection to us, because we have shown that we cannot handle them. Today and forever more, we need to constantly put our emotions into subjection under the Word of YAH.

Allow our thoughts and our actions to be weighed in how they will please our Elohim, and how they will affect His kingdom. If our thoughts are not going to edify and bring forth fruit, then our thoughts are outside of His will, and we need to seek His face in order to understand how He would have us carry out this matter. If we do not immediately see a way to constructively express ourselves, then maybe what we are trying to invest in the situation is not necessary. As women it is time to jump off the daily emotional rollercoaster, and walk in the light of love, righteousness, and truth. We will no longer be in fear of being walked over if we let something slide. We will not feel weak if our rebuke of offenses are handed to the Father. We don't have to be in control, and submit to the perception that has been given to us about our emotional state. We will be unwavering and steadfast as our Abba ministers to us through His Word. We will hold our tongue, and when we do speak, we let our words drip with honey, so we are not overlooked or misunderstood, because of our emotions. Acting in our strength profits nothing, but relying on the WORD, and being silent gives Yah an opportunity to fight our battles, and heal our hurts.

Scripture Reading:

Wherefore, my beloved brethren, let every man be swift to hear, slow to speak, slow to wrath:

James 1:19 (KJV)

He that is slow to wrath is of great understanding: but he that is hasty of spirit exalteth folly.

Proverbs 14:29 (KJV)

Better is the end of a thing than the beginning thereof: and the patient in spirit is better than the proud in spirit.

Ecclesiastes 7:8 (KJV)

But the fruit of the Spirit is love, joy, peace, long suffering, gentleness, goodness, faith, Meekness, temperance: against such there is no law. And they that are Messiah's have crucified the flesh with the affections and lusts. If we live in the Spirit, let us also walk in the Spirit. Let us not be desirous of vain glory, provoking one another, envying one another.

Galatians 5:22-26 (KJV)

DAY: SEVEN

Repentance

For after my turning back I repented,
and after coming to understand I struck my thigh.
I was ashamed and also humiliated,
because I bore the disgrace of my youth.
Jeremiah 31:19

When we are called to this walk of faith, we are being beckoned first to repent. Our repentance is the first badge on our scout jackets for HaMashiach (Hebrew for the Messiah). Our repentance shows our devotion, and that we have chosen to follow the Master. The biblical definition of repentance is not just confessing, nor is it just asking for forgiveness. True repentance is a change of direction from a path leading to destruction, and a returning to a path of life. Before the foundation of the earth the plan of redemption for humanity was already established. The plan of salvation would provide a way for each of us to return to the Father, and seek out His path.

If you have been walking on your own path, turn around, and look for His narrow path that has life and blessings. Today, seek the path of the Father without reservation. On this path is restoration and rest from our wandering. It is only on this path that we have the opportunity to return like the prodigal child did back to his father's house. In the house of our Abba is protection. Under the rules of His house are where we receive His blessings. As we seek the Father, let us remember that the only call is a return to Him. It is not simply a return to a church building. It is not finding

41

a short cut or a different path. It is in His way, and according to His will that we have the opportunity to be restored from our wayward ways.

> *If my people, which are called by my name, shall humble themselves, and pray, and seek my face, and turn from their wicked ways; then will I hear from heaven, and will forgive their sin, and will heal their land.*
>
> 2 Chronicles 7:14 (KJV)

Scripture Reading:

> *From that time Yeshua began to preach, and to say, Repent: for the Kingdom of heaven is at hand.*
>
> Matthew 4:17 (KJV)

> *In those days came John the Baptist, preaching in the wilderness of Judaea, And saying, Repent ye: for the Kingdom of heaven is at hand. For this is He that was spoken of by the prophet Esaias, saying, The voice of one crying in the wilderness, Prepare ye the way of Yahuah, make his paths straight. And the same John had his raiment of camel's hair, and a leathern girdle about his loins; and his meat was locusts and wild honey. Then went out to him Jerusalem, and all Judaea, and all the region round about Jordan, And were baptized of him in Jordan, confessing their sins. But when He saw many of the Pharisees and Sadducees come to his baptism, He said unto them, O generation of vipers, who hath warned you to flee from the wrath to come? Bring forth therefore fruits meet for repentance: And think not to say within yourselves, We have Abraham to our father: for I say unto you, that God is able of these stones to raise up children unto Abraham. And now also the axe is laid unto the root of the trees: therefore every tree*

which bringeth not forth good fruit is hewn down, and cast into the fire.

Matthew 3:1-10 (KJV)

Read Isaiah 5:1-24

DAY: EIGHT

Threshing Floor

But they do not know the thoughts of YHWH,
and they do not understand his plan,
that He has gathered them as sheaves
to his threshing floor.
Micah 4:12

The people of the Most High have been scattered in the wind because of their disobedience. Scattered and lost are two different things. Yahuah has never lost a sheep, and though it seems like a trying time around the world for His chosen people (who have been scattered to the four corners) it is not the end. The prophecies of His people have not all been fulfilled, and as He has stated various times throughout scripture, He has not forsaken the remnant (Romans 11:5). From slavery to eugenics, there has been a plan to eradicate the people of Yah from the face of the earth. All of this affliction is not without rhyme or reason, but it is because of idolatry and stiff necks that these things have been allowed. Yet even out of His chastisement, we are currently living in the time of a mass awakening. People all over the world are returning to the precepts and commandments of the Most High. Hearts are being humbled, and once again many of us are seeking His face. This is the generation of those who seek Him (Psalm 24:6), but from the outside there looks to be more calamity than comfort for this noble change of heart.

The reason why we don't immediately experience the joy of our salvation is because the transformation from our image to His is not always easy for us. First we must be gathered and separated on His threshing floor.

We have entered the time of the separation of the wheat from the tare. Many of us have spent so much time looking like the other religious groups around us with our man made customs and practices, that it has become hard to differentiate between a true believer and a person who delights merely in traditional religious observances. Because of this, we are being gathered to the threshing floor for separation.

In ancient culture the threshing floor was a well known place. The threshing floor is where the wheat was taken and laid out on the floor. The wheat was then trampled by oxen until the grain was loosened from its husk. After the grain was loosened from the husk, wind or winnowing would be used to blow or toss the chaff and straw away where it could be gathered for fire. The act of threshing releases the edible part of a grain from the stock. The same is true of the heart of His beloved. In order to get to the usable part of the heart it needs to be broken. The breaking of the tough outer shell reveals the tenderest part which is good for use.

Yah is taking us and applying pressure to release the part of us that is usable for His kingdom. Don't be like the chaff blown away from the threshing floor by every wind of man-made doctrine. We must hold fast. It is not until we submit to the threshing floor of Yah that we can truly experience who we are meant to be. Allow Yah to separate you. As the strong and experienced Ox who is used to , He is an expert thresher who has never lost a grain. And as the wise gardener He has never mixed a wheat with a tare. He has a keen eye and is not applying pressure to destroy you, but He is removing your former self to allow the world to see that you have been different all along. Withstand the pressure of your separation, because it is on the threshing floor where Yah is working out His change in you.

Scripture Reading:

Read the Book of Ruth

DAY: NINE

Obedience

Is there as much delight for YHWH in burnt offerings and sacrifices
as there is in obeying YHWH?
Look! To obey is better than sacrifice;
to give heed than the fat of rams.
1 Samuel 15:22 (LEB)

Many people, in a recent move back to the Hebrew culture
and context of scripture, have decided to obey the Most High. In
doing so there has been much objection from religious groups
around the world. There have been accusations of becoming
jew"ish," rumors of falling away from belief in Messiah, and ultimately being called a cult. All that being said, the opinions of
man and how they feel about a believers devotion and obedience
to their Elohim can be disheartening to say the least. This type of
persecution gives a whole new meaning to being persecuted for
His names sake.

> *Blessed are ye, when men shall revile you, and perse-
> cute you, and shall say all manner of evil against you
> falsely, for my sake.*

Matthew 5:11

This walk has not been a wake-up-in-the-morning type
process. The soil of my heart has been prepared from my mother's womb and what is manifesting now is the fruit of cultivation.
The negative and positive have all been for the chance to stand
with Him. Early in my walk I desired lots of guidance. I sought

49

books, mentors, and other people dedicated to ministry. I attended conferences on faith, but all this never quenched the thirst and desire that I had inside to have a deeper relationship with the Most High. At one conference there was a pastor's wife who was a keynote speaker. She began talking about how our lives are to be a reflection of the Messiah. She used the illustration of Muhammed Ali and Will Smith. She stated how Will Smith for his role in "Ali," followed the legend around and watched his every move. She stated that he even went as far as to try and talk like him. The speaker said they would go back and forth saying "float like a butterfly sting like a bee," this was conveyed to go on for a while until one day they did the exercise and Muhammed Ali couldn't tell his voice from Will Smith's. The speaker concluded that our lives were supposed to be like that with Messiah. After spending time with Him; our walk, talk, and actions should reflect Him. She emphatically stated that we want to be so close to Him that when people see us, they see Him. Her words resonated my heart and instantly created a need for action.

That day was the day that I decided my walk would not be that of a hearer, but a doer also. My seeking was not for books, conferences, or mentors any longer. My desire was to sit at the feet of the Master and learn from Him. While I am sure my walk may not have been her intention, it was that speech, and those words that set fire to my soul. Sometimes the words of those around us, even when they don't understand the purpose, are meant to take us to the next level spiritually. I learned that day that what YHWH wants from me is my life as a living sacrifice. What He wants is a willing vessel. What He desires of me is not my intentions, but my actions. He wants me to yearn and strive to reflect His Word. In order to achieve this I have to do something. I have to change. I cannot make excuses for my imperfections or half heartedly seek Him. I must want to dwell in His presence so that when He sees me He sees a reflection of Himself. As a child of the Most High we want to resemble our Father and we do so by having a heart for His Word and following what it says.

Scripture Reading:

> Yeshua answered and said unto him, If a man love me, He will keep my words: and my Father will love him, and we will come unto him, and make our abode with him.

John 14:23 (KJV)

Read Entire Chapter of Deuteronomy 28

DAY: TEN

Prayer

YHWH is nigh unto all them that call upon him, to all that call upon him in truth.
Psalm 145:18

So many people today are using prayer as a form of witch-craft. Yes, I said witchcraft. It is being treated like a magic string of words and commands in order to receive some type of gift from an unseen realm. Can you see it now? The Western idea of prayer is completely egocentric, and has absolutely nothing to do with the original intent our Abba (Father) had for prayer. Prayer isn't talking to some mysterious "God" sitting far away in order to pep talk him into bestowing something upon you. Prayer is so much deeper. Prayer is actually meditation.

If we look into the Eastern culture we will see a shadow of what prayer was like in Biblical times. While there have been pre-visions at the hands of mankind, what we see in Eastern culture is a lot more realistic than closing our eyes and telling Santa...I mean "YHWH" what we want for Christmas...I mean...oops. You see how twisted it is now, don't you? Prayer has become like Al-addin, but with unlimited wishes. Now that we have viewed prayer from a deductive position, let us now view it in its proper cultural and spiritual context.

Prayer is the joining together of the mind and the spirit. Prayer is meditating on the essence of YHWH before you ask for anything, and finally prayer provides introspection. The last part of that is the most beautiful part. It tells us what prayer is for and why Yah gave it to us. Prayer is a gift and in prayer and meditation we often find the answer to what we are looking for, not because there is a magic formula to unlocking the vault of YHWH's riches, because that is not what prayer is for (If you want the riches of YHWH we will cover that in obedience). Prayer is the gift and ability to be able to look into one's self in a private setting with just you and the Most High. Prayer is an ability to evaluate who and where you are in your walk and your obedience to His Word. Prayer is where we are laid bare and are asking for guidance in our next move toward a more consistent understanding of the world around us and our purpose in it. It's not about getting but actually what can we put forth in order to produce the change we want to see. Prayer is not for needs, because our Heavenly Father has already provided those, and prayer is not for our wants because we would already have them if we were walking in obedience. Prayer is a look into the deepest part of ourselves with the desire to manifest into the type of person who will benefit the Kingdom. Prayer is where we transcend and allow for spiritual rejuvenation so we can continue on this walk. Prayer is the place where we come face to face with the Living Elohim and don't die, but are given the opportunity to be nourished with His love. Prayer is not the place to ask, but in prayer is where we are getting all we need. Prayer is where the will of Yah is met with our desire to do what He has put before us. It is only the prayers that are in His will that He will even hear.

Let us be careful that we not pray for carnal things, rather let us remember that it is YHWH's will that we pray. Amen.

Scripture Reading:

Rejoice evermore. Pray without ceasing. In everything give thanks: for this is the will of Yah in Yeshua our Messiah concerning you.

I Thessalonians 5:16-18 (KJV)

And this is the confidence that we have in him, that, if we ask any thing according to His will, He heareth us:

1 John 5:14 (KJV)

Read Entire Chapter of Jeremiah 29

DAY: ELEVEN

Forgiveness

For if ye forgive men their trespasses, your heavenly Father will also forgive you:
But if ye forgive not men their trespasses, neither will your Father forgive your
trespasses.
Matthew 6:14-15

Forgiving is something we all say we have done, but in reality we don't even know where to begin. Without a proper understanding of what forgiveness is how could we have ever done so? I don't know about everyone, but for me this reality hit me like a ton of bricks. Have I really forgiven those that have trespassed against me? I have been saying the Master's Prayer ("Lord's" Prayer, Matthew 6:9-13), in Hebrew from memory for over a few months now, and have recently realized I have just been reciting in vain, the words "and forgive us our debt as we forgive our debtors." Was I really speaking with lying lips unknowingly? The answer is yes! I was being a HYPOCRITE. Standing in front of a room full of people with words that have never permeated the stone of my unforgiving heart. Forgiveness isn't easy, and that's no cop out, it's the truth. The reality is that the only people who we have a problem forgiving are the ones closest to us, because no one else can hurt us the way they can. I have watched plenty of estranged relationships, whether it was mother and daughter, son and father, husband and wife, and do you know what the common denominator in all these relationships are? LOVE. Deep Love. The only relationship that can birth the amount of un-forgiveness that many of us have comes from a place of deep rooted love. When we love people we expect them to protect us and never end up at the receiving end of our forgiveness. But what happens when they have wronged us? What happens when they have denied us the very love we have invested? What happens when they don't protect us? What happens when they say or do things that make us doubt their devotion? What do we do at that point? What do we do when we are abandoned in the pits of life waiting for someone to see that we are wounded? Maybe five minutes before I wrote this I didn't know the answer to that question either. I have read the Bible, I have studied the commentaries, I have searched the Psalms, but today in the language that my Savior spoke I was able to see for the first time why my heart has been so heavy. It's because I wasn't forgiving, but I was keeping a record of wrong. In order to forgive there is action involved, and I was not willing to do the very thing that would set me free.

Forgiveness, in Hebrew means to lift a burden or to lift a load off. Forgiveness means to let go and to feel lighter. Forgiveness means, leave it behind. Forgiveness doesn't mean to carry and hold for a later time when I can make you feel like you have made me feel. Forgiveness doesn't mean reciprocate or recompense. Forgiveness means to pardon. It means yes, you are guilty, and no, an apology won't suffice, but I know that the burden of what you did isn't mine to carry and instead of waiting around for the other person to take responsibility and retrieve their burden off my back, I will take the loss. I will leave that burden behind, because the loss of holding on to my offense is greater than losing the relationship that I so dearly want to preserve. It also may require letting go so that a person is not occupying space in my heart that they don't deserve. Instead of letting the dead weight of old offenses hold us back, it is time to lay them at the brazen alter. Offenses and hurts are entirely too heavy to tote through life's journey, and in reality it will only keep us from experiencing the love and joy that Yah has stored away for us. Today as we forgive we are making room for all the blessings that our unforgiveness is blocking.

My Prayer for you today:

Today I ask that Yah lifts the burden of an unforgiving heart. I ask that He gives you peace and finally allows you to be released from the bondage of bitterness and unforgiveness. I pray that you stop waiting for your chance to recompense them what they deserve, forgive them of that debt, and release them from the prison of your heart and mind where they are taking up space. I ask that the Most High will fill that space with His love and peace, and that you will become a vessel that can be used as a testimony of forgiveness for his Kingdom. AMEN.

Scripture Reading:

I, even I, am He that blotteth out thy transgressions for mine own sake, and will not remember thy sins. Put me in remembrance: let us plead together: declare thou, that thou mayest be justified.
Isaiah 43:25-26

And every priest standeth daily ministering and offering oftentimes the same sacrifices, which can never take away sins: But this man, after He had offered one sacrifice for sins forever, sat down on the right hand of God; From henceforth expecting till his enemies be made his footstool. For by one offering He hath perfected forever them that are sanctified. Whereof the Ruach HaQodesh (Holy Ghost) also is a witness to us: for after that He had said before, This is the covenant that I will make with them after those days, saith Yahuah, I will put my laws into their hearts, and in their minds will I write them; And their sins and iniquities will I remember no more.

Hebrews 10:11-17 (KJV)

Read Matthew 18:21-35

DAY: TWELVE

Forgotten Paths

For My people have forgotten Me, They burn incense to worthless gods And they have stumbled from their ways, From the ancient paths, To walk in bypaths, Not on a highway,
Jeremiah 18:15

What good would a steering wheel be if we couldn't use it to turn around when we are going in the wrong direction? Sometimes our pride removes the luxury of the proverbial steering wheel from our lives. Just like our ancestors and the individuals in scripture, our inability to use this tool has constantly baffled the Most High. In His Word, He gives us so many options to getting back onto the right path, and they all start with returning to Him. He is willing to step in and steer us back in the right direction. Like a Carrie Underwood karaoke moment, let us all belt out "Yah! TAKE THE WHEEL." Now while that was easy, it seems to be much harder actually allowing Him to do so. We become so comfortable with our routine and our earthly pleasures that we remain stagnant in ministry, in work, and in our homes. It is much easier to keep doing the same thing rather than doing something different or returning back to the way we know is right. What would we say of a hiker who started off on a trail that was only supposed to be 30 minutes to their destination and after almost 2 hours hadn't reached it? What if this hiker just kept walking as it became darker and darker in the woods hoping that by just walking they would end up at their desired destination? The same is true of us. While it is light we are walking in the wrong direction, but the night time is coming, and in the darkest hour of our lives we often find ourselves so lost that we can't even see our own hands. We become unrecognizable even to ourselves. In these moments we need Yah more than ever to take the wheel. This is the time where we need Him to shine His light onto our path and be a lamp to our feet so we can stop, turn around, and head back in the right direction. It is His Word and the path of righteousness that is the call of His chosen. Let us not forget Him, let us not turn to the gods of this world and their customs, but let us rely on the Word to shine light in our lives and reveals the things that have taken us into the night of life and caused us to stumble in the way. Once He has illuminated the dark places of our hearts where, we store our idols, I pray, in humility we turn back to the ancient and sure path where there is light and life, and forsake that which causes us to stray.

Scripture Reading:

> I have heard what the prophets said, that prophesy lies in my name, saying, I have dreamed, I have dreamed. How long shall this be in the heart of the prophets that prophesy lies? Yea, they are prophets of the deceit of their own heart; Which think to cause my people to forget my name by their dreams which they tell every man to his neighbour, as their fathers have forgotten my name for Baal.
>
> Jeremiah 23:25-27 (KJV)

But Jeshurun waxed fat, and kicked: thou art waxen fat, thou art grown thick, thou art covered with fatness; then He forsook God which made him, and lightly esteemed the Rock of his salvation. They provoked him to jealousy with strange gods, with abominations provoked they him to anger. They sacrificed unto devils, not to God; to gods whom they knew not, to new gods that came newly up, whom your fathers feared not. Of the Rock that begat thee thou art unmindful, and hast forgotten God that formed thee.

Deuteronomy 32:15-18 (KJV)

And the children of Israel did evil in the sight of Yahuah, and forgat Yahuah their Elohim, and served Baalim and the groves.

Judges 3:7 (KJV)

Even from the days of your fathers ye are gone away from mine ordinances, and have not kept them. Return unto me, and I will return unto you, saith Yahuah of hosts. But ye said, Wherein shall we return?

Malachi 3:7 (KJV)

DAY: THIRTEEN

Restoration

Whom the heaven must receive until the times of restitution of all things, which YHWH hath spoken by the mouth of all his holy prophets since the world began.
Acts 3:21

The strong delusion of the last days and the great falling away is happening right before our eyes, and as mothers we have to be on guard. Our seed, the one we have been entrusted with to nurture and shield is under attack. In the physical realm we may only get a glimpse of the attacks, that is until we start to look at things through the Father's eyes. Through the Father's eyes we are facing principalities and darkness. It is only through His light that we are able to shield ourselves, and those around us for the consuming horror of a life away from the Father. All of these attacks have a base root and they can be seen in the beginning.

In the Garden of Eden, Chawah (the mother of all living), the true name of the first woman, (not Eve as we have in English), was deceived, not Adam (1 Tim. 2:14). For years the fall has been worn as a badge that marks women for oppression and mistreatment, thus perpetuating exactly what Satan's plan was from the beginning. Satan choosing Chawah was because of her future influence. Satan, like a master chess player, is always several steps ahead in his plan. While he has no victory in the end he constantly wins little battles by defeating us with our own biases. The reality of the situation is that Satan didn't want Adam. He wanted the woman. Through deeper Hebrew study, and a thorough survey of scripture, we find out that he wanted her because she had a special and important job. Her job was to house and protect the seed. This seed was not just the physical seed, but the seed of truth and righteousness. If Satan could get the man and woman to be at ought, He could own the seed and never allow them to become one in mind, body, and spirit. This discord kills the picture of family. If Satan could get the man to rule over and dominate the woman, the woman would rebel, and like a domino effect she would teach her children to be rebellious. A rebellious seed is a corrupt seed, and a corrupt seed will never bear good fruit.

Many of our homes, blended families, and associates bear mixed fruit. We have sown seed of corruption because we have tried to lead in our own power. The men are ruling with an iron fist and the women are haughty and rebellious, but all the while the seed is observing. We are doing a great job of fulfilling Satan's plan to corrupt the seed. It is time to allow Yah to make amends in our homes. The Hebrew word for wholeness is shalom, but the word for amends is Shalam. There can be no wholeness until amends have been made. Instead of perpetuating the curses of our forefathers, let us repent for them and seek out the harmony that brings shalom. Instead of demanding submission and change from our partners, let us both submit to Yah and allow Him to do the rest. Selfish plans need to be put on hold so we can sow seeds of righteousness. We need to remove the bitterness, anger, accusation, and disappointment from our hearts and allow Yah to fix the most sacred institution on the planet, our families. If your parents failed, your reasonable service is to do better with your children. Do not perpetuate generational cycles that are not profitable to the Kingdom. Just because we are fallen doesn't mean we can forsake the original intent for marriage and family relationships. Marriage is a picture of Yahoshua and the called out congregation, and family is a picture of the called out and their companions. The picture is that of oneness (echad). Just because Adam had to toil doesn't mean he was never supposed to work the ground, that's how his Family would eat. Likewise, just because a wife would strive for her husband doesn't mean that we are not supposed to do the best we can to seek Yah and unity so we can stop the generational curses, and raise up righteous seed. It's not impossible because it has happened in the lives of those who were faithful. Forty-Two generations of women and men forsook generational curses and raised up men and women who sought the face of Yah, and because of their obedience we received a Messiah who redeemed the world from sin and death. The same is needed in the latter days. The future of our walk and families are dependent on our selflessness. Now is the time to pay restitution and to do it right. Let us fix the trespass of sacred things so our seed will bear fruit of our amends. Let us be the picture of a garden that brings forth good fruit in due season.

Scripture Reading:

And I will restore to you the years that the locust hath eaten, the cankerworm, and the caterpiller, and the palmerworm, my great army which I sent among you. And ye shall eat in plenty, and be satisfied, and praise the name of Yahuah your God, that hath dealt wondrously with you: and my people shall never be ashamed.

Joel 2:25-26 (KJV)

Restore unto me the joy of thy salvation; and uphold me with thy free spirit.

Psalm 51:12 (KJV)

Read Entire Chapter of Acts 3

DAY: FOURTEEN

Learn His Ways

It is written in the prophets, And they shall be all taught of Yah. Every man therefore that hath heard, and hath learned of the Father, cometh unto me.
John 6:45

Waiting for the Messiah has lost its meaning. When most people think about waiting they envision sitting and doing nothing as time passes. While that seems really relaxing it is not what the Biblical writers, nor Yehoshua had in mind when He left to prepare a place for us. As the bride of our Messiah he has a special desire for us to be actively waiting for him. This type of waiting requires preparation. Just like a bride planning a wedding requires effort, so does our preparation for meeting our Bridegroom.

In Western culture we have it quite backwards when it comes to weddings. The bride often does all the planning and preparing, and the groom just shows up. The complete opposite is true of Hebrew customs. In the Hebrew custom the man and His Family took care of the arrangements. The only thing the bride and her family were responsible for was making sure she stayed pure until her marriage. After the betrothal, the groom usually went back to his home country until an appointed time. The bride was not privy to when the groom would return. During this time the bride's family would be teaching her how to be a wife. An important part of this process, especially right before the marriage ceremony, was the purification and anointing of the bride.

In many ancient Eastern cultures, marriage comes with a purification ritual. It is not only physical, it is also symbolic. The bride is cleansed and anointed for her husband. She is presented as a prize for her groom. She is his and ONLY his (1 Cor. 6:19-20). The same is true for us as the Bride of Messiah (Christ). We are in our purification process. When He came and died He paid his dowry to sin and death. He finished His work, which was payment for His bride in full at His resurrection. His work is finished, but ours has just begun. We are to be continually washed and anointed with His WORD. He wants us to forget our people, our customs, and our ways, and look to His people, His customs and His ways. As a good bride, our desire should be to learn our future husband. We should inquire of His father what He likes to eat, what breaks His heart, and what He desires of us so when we are presented to Him at the great wedding feast we can be pleasing to Him. The Messiah has done His part and He is now waiting for us to do ours. Let us learn His ways so that, as a beautiful bride we can stand before Him ready to serve for eternity.

> Let us be glad and rejoice, and give honour to him: for the marriage of the Lamb is come, and his wife hath made herself ready. And to her was granted that she should be arrayed in fine linen, clean and white: for the fine linen is the righteousness of saints.
> Revelation 19:7-8

Scripture Reading:

It is good for me that I have been afflicted; that I might learn thy statutes. The law of thy mouth is better unto me than thousands of gold and silver. Thy hands have made me and fashioned me: give me understanding, that I may learn thy commandments.

Psalm 119:71-73 (KJV)

It is written in the prophets, And they shall be all taught of Yah. Every man therefore that hath heard, and hath learned of the Father, cometh unto me.

John 6:45 (KJV)

Take my yoke upon you, and learn of me; for I am meek and lowly in heart: and ye shall find rest unto your souls.

Matthew 11:29 (KJV)

Wherewithal shall a young man cleanse his way? by taking heed thereto according to thy word.

Psalm 119:9 (KJV)

DAY: FIFTEEN

The Womb

I was cast upon thee from the womb: thou art my Elohim from my mother's belly.
Psalm 22:10

We never picture Yah as having feminine attributes. Often times in our Western minds we forget that Yah is Spirit, and that as The Great I AM, He embodies everything. It is He who breathes the first breath of life into humans. He gives a safe place for the life to be nurtured often secured from all those who seek to do us harm. Like a mother, He places us in the proverbial womb of His protection allowing for growth.

While we are in our growth process He is constantly giving us nourishment. He gives all first, and in return for His giving we are expected to put Him first. Many parents demand the same of their children, quoting how they carried and nurtured them so to get disrespect in exchange for their selflessness is unacceptable. If an earthly parent can demand honor for their duty to their child, how much more can Yahuah?

Yah carried Israel in the womb of the wilderness where they practiced for the Promise Land. In the womb there is protection from harm. Breathing is practiced without the pressure of gravity against fragile lungs. The same with following Yah. In the wilderness Yah was protecting Israel from the outside influences as they learned how to live and breathe the instructions of Torah. It wasn't until they were birthed or placed into the Promise Land that the practical teaching of the wilderness journey had such significant meaning. When Yah left the enemies to prove Israel's devotion it was finally time to see what they were "made" of. There was no longer the safety of the womb, but now what had been grown and cultivated as a strong nation was forced to fully experience the elements of the outside world pressing on every side.

Many of us are like Israel, we have left the womb of comfort. Maybe you have started a new journey. Maybe you have taken the next step in your walk of faith, and are now having to put the lessons of the Bible into practice. The reality is that Yah would not have moved you to this point without believing you were equipped. This is the time now to prove your devotion to this walk. As the master teacher steps back to watch his star pupil, likewise will Yah stand back and watch you carry out His will as His chosen. You have the tools. You have the practical knowledge. Now is time to let your light shine. As you come face to face with opposition stand firm and declare that you are following the one who has nurtured you and not those around you who only seek to devour you.

Scripture Reading:

> We are troubled on every side, yet not distressed; we are perplexed, but not in despair; Persecuted, but not forsaken; cast down, but not destroyed;
>
> 2 Corinthians 4:8-9 (KJV)

> As one whom his mother comforteth, so will I comfort you; and ye shall be comforted in Jerusalem.
>
> Isaiah 66:13 (KJV)

Can a woman forget her sucking child, that she should not have compassion on the son of her womb? yea, they may forget, yet will I not forget thee.

Isaiah 49:15 (KJV)

DAY: SIXTEEN

Play Your Role

Likewise, ye wives, be in subjection to your own husbands; that, if any obey not the word, they also may without the word be won by the conversation of the wives.

1 Peter 3:1

In our modern culture we have been indoctrinated that men and women are the same in all ways. In the early years of the Women's Liberation Movement, women propagated the thought that "anything he can do I can do better." They burned their bras, shaved their heads, and set out to leave the home and make their own way just like their male counterparts.

Today we witness the residual effects of an abandoned post. As women, we strive for promotions to higher positions with long hours, we aspire to overthrow the rule of a male "dominant" society, and all this is done in order to prove that "YHWH" made us for the same purposes and with the same thought in mind. The truth of the matter, and I know many people will hate me for saying this but...man and woman were not created for the same purpose. Now before you label me as an anti feminist and a weak woman; hear me out.

Roles are a very important part of our society. At our jobs there is hierarchy set up and some positions can be obtained through hard work and some are inherent and no matter how hard you try it just won't happen. (Before I make my point remember there are always special-case scenarios, but in this case, we are talking about in a normal situation.)

Example: You work for a major company. For argument sake, let's say Ford. You start off as a factory worker. Through hard work you become a manager and eventually you become the CEO. Although CEO is a high and respected job, you are still not a Ford heir.

When all is said and done the inherent rule of the company belongs to the family and its share holders. You are at the top but even at the top there is hierarchy and order. This order is not something that demotes or makes the CEO less important, but actually it solidifies the position. When it comes to the relationship between men and women there is order and the order is set up to solidify the position of everyone in this system. Don't believe me? Let's look at it.

Before Yahuah (YHWH) created anything He made order. The order was Salvation, the Aleph-Tav, a home, lights, food, THEN man. Once man was created He made sure that He had all these things to offer (food, clothing, shelter, and a job) before He brought woman in the picture. There again was order.

When Yah (YHWH) brings the woman she is sent as a help to man. He doesn't create a separate home, job etc. for her in order for her to be appealing to man. Neither is the choice left to her on whether or not she needs the things that man has to offer. The order is set up so that all that man has to offer is similar to all the things that YHWH had already set up for man. She is coming into a prepared situation. She is coming to carry out a particular function within a divine structure. But the situation is not one of leisure, and the form and function of her duty is not to be looked down upon. She is the keeper (1 Timothy 5:14, Titus 2:5) of the home. She carries out all the business of the home as her husband deals with the weighty matters of diplomacy and global affairs.

Our jobs as women is to build a legacy. We have the first chance with every child who comes through the matrix. We also have the chance to pursue our personal dreams and goals. While the man's job is fixed, ours is left up to our own creativity and imagination. We are not created to be linear and only carry out one task from the cradle to the grave. We were given the opportunity to explore, and the only requirement was that at the end of the day we put our Most High and His Torah first, husbands second, and family after Him, thus allowing us to be One (ehad).

As we go out into the cutthroat world this week and operate as the Proverb 31 woman (working) from home or not, remember that home is first. Our submission to our calling should be met with the same seriousness that we take the orders from our bosses at work. Also, remember the time we invest in our children is an important legacy. Remember, our husbands need us as a comforter and a quiet solace from the perils of this wicked world. Build up our men, love them, encourage them, and support them. Instead of coveting his position let's begin today by embracing our own. It was the nations with a strong family foundation who thrived. Let us learn from our ancestors and handle first things first. Let's fulfill our job, and by doing so we put our kings back on their throne. By doing so in obedience to Yah's Word we are allowed to take our seats next to them as their queens.

Scripture Reading:

Read Entire Chapter of Proverbs 31

DAY: SEVENTEEN

Hurt

When my heart was embittered
and I felt stabbed in my kidneys,
then I was brutish and ignorant.
Psalm 73:21-22

My husband has had a couple of really bad bouts with kidney stones. During his experience, I listened to him and others share stories about the pain they felt when they were going through the process of passing the stones. Men and women alike both compared it to the worst pain they had ever experienced (even worse than child birth). I remember the last set of kidney stones my husband passed like it was yesterday. I remember the agonizing cry for help, and the plea for death that was never going to come.

"Hurt" in the ancient Hebrew is likened to that of being stabbed in the kidneys. Having our feelings hurt, and emotions toyed around with is some of the worst pain we will ever experience. In our pain we often seek relief, but there is beauty in our pain. The beauty in our pain is the lesson. The ability to be taught something. It almost seems cruel, but a lesson that has adversity sticks with the human mind much better than one carried in it reward.

Sometimes Yah allows us to experience hurt in order to teach us a lesson. As the psalmist wrote there is a lot of transparency about his indignant feelings, but the one thing that remained constant was that he, in all of his pain, anguish, and bitterness had Yah. Oh how painful to be stricken in the kidneys and have no hope. As believers we have a High Priest who has been through the same pain we have been through. When we experience separation, loss of loved ones, or betrayal it is easy to feel like we are all alone. But as followers, when we go before the throne we are face to face with the Master who knows our pain. Our pain means so much to Him that He was willing to lay down His life to secure a place for us in eternity. Praise Yah that although we face obstacles that will surely hurt us in this life, He is there and has not forsaken us.

Scripture Reading:

> And they put away the strange gods from among them, and served Yahuah: and his soul was grieved for the misery of Israel.
>
> Judges 10:16 (KJV)

> Now all these things happened unto them for examples: and they are written for our admonition, upon whom the ends of the world are come.
>
> 1 Corinthians 10:11 (KJV)

DAY: EIGHTEEN

Keep It!

"If you love me, you will keep my commandments.
John 14:15

"If." The looming conjunction that is always followed by some type of conditional obligation. Whether we want to admit it or not, there are conditions in relationships that are attached to their success. At work there are rules. In marriage there are vows which carry conditions. While our culture may want to believe that our love is unconditional, the reality is everything we do is based in condition. Even the infinite one Himself gives conditions for our relationship with Him.

People in Christendom are under the grave misconception that because "Jesus has paid it all" they have to do nothing. Theologians have convinced the world that doing anything is working for your salvation, even though in the Book of James we are called to work out our salvation (James 2:14-26). While I am not saying you can earn anything, I am implying that there is more to be done than lip service (Philippians 2:12). These inconsistencies show that the masses have been fooled into lawlessness by man's interpretation of YHWH's Word.

The very things we were warned about by Messiah have come true and many of us are failing to stand firm in the face of opposition to truth. Our comfort zones and our traditions are standing between us and the narrow path of righteousness (Matthew 7:12-14). We have clergy cheerleaders who shout behind us as we walk opposite of our Example. Anytime we even mention feeling unsure about the path they are promoting we are sung a lullaby and put back to sleep with nice words about just resting in Messiah's finished work. But what if I told you that a half truth is still a whole lie?

In Western religion we can do no wrong. We have no real rules, and we can sin as long as we don't have sex (which isn't a sin, fornication and adultery are), drink (which isn't a sin, being drunk is), or hang out with sinners (which Messiah did). The religious world has made up their own set of laws and have forsaken the laws and precepts of the Most High Elohim. It seems the only time we even turn to the "Old" Testament is when it is time to collect tithes and offerings, or for YHWH's promises and blessings.

While it may be hard to stomach, it is undeniably evident that all of His promises and blessings in the Old and New Testament have conditions. His conditions are interwoven into His covenants. When we are in covenant we are compelled to behave differently. For instance, when you are married you no longer behave like you are single. The same is true for our walk. When we were without an Elohim, we lived like we didn't have one, but now that we have one we are to show evidence and fruit of this relationship (Ephesians 2:12).

Messiah told us He doesn't speak His own words, but only what the Father has said (John 12:49). He also told us He wants us to keep His commandments. In keeping those commandments we are showing our love for Him. Now here's the condition, what about when we don't? "He that loveth me not keepeth not my sayings: and the word which ye hear is not mine, but the Father's which sent me" (John 14:24). If we say we love Messiah and we don't keep the word He was sent by Yah to give us, then we do not love Him. Obedience is evidence of our new life in Messiah. If He is obedient and He is our example then likewise we should follow Him in obedience. Let us instead of being hearers of the Word, be doers also (James 1:22). Let us guard His Word in our hearts so we don't sin against Him (Psalm 119:11). Let us walk in truth when we say we love Him. Let us learn of Him. Let us forsake man in all things, and draw near unto the author and finisher of our faith for guidance. Let us take the scripture for what it is first, before we allow anyone to convince us otherwise. The psalmist wrote "Thy righteousness is an everlasting righteousness, and thy law is the truth" (Psalm 119:142). Because Yah is omnipotent, we cannot fool Him. He knows our innermost being; so let us be truthful in our walk lest we fall under the condemnation of 1 John 2:4. "He that saith, I know him, and keepeth not his commandments, is a liar, and the truth is not in him." Let us seek the face of Yah today and ask HIM, by studying His whole WORD, what it is He wants us to do. Because, at the end of the day, we serve an audience of One.

Additional Thought and Reading:

At the great day of judgment when we stand before the Eternal One, the only question He will ask is what did you do with my WORD (my Only Begotten). If we say we believed in Him, but did not do as He told us to do, will that be enough? (Revelation 20:13).

My prayer today is that you "error" on the side of answering that you followed His WORD, and did what He said to the best of your ability, rather than saying your pastor, mother, father, etc. said you didn't have to do anything, so you didn't even try.

Read Matthew 25:14-30

DAY: NINETEEN

Messy Ministry

And let us not be weary in well doing: for in due season we shall reap, if we faint not.
Galatians 6:9

For several years I have been passionate about blogging/writing, but my passion always seemed to be met with opposition and a lack of passion when adversity hits. I'm sure many of you can relate. Everything in life seems to be flowing just the way you like and then everything stops. It's almost like someone threw on the emergency break while you were going 100 miles per hour. I mean an abrupt halt. A halt of information, a halt of inspiration, a halt of determination. In the beginning of my writing journey everything was contingent upon how I felt or how people received what it was I was saying. My writing was mine and I took everything about it very personal. If opposition or inspiration stopped, so did I.

It was so bad that, five years ago (around the time I first got the message from Yah that blogging/ writing would be a part of my ministry) I would have perceived a road block as a sign that things were not going well and would have closed up shop. I would have seen lack of inspiration as reason to abort mission and find something else to embark upon. five years later, and five years more experienced, I realize something about ministry and mission...it's messy business. Not messy in terms of negativity and drama, but messy as in hard work and sometimes chaotic. I have learned from my mom (my muse if you please) that not all chaos is without order.

Growing up (and even now) my mom will have 50 million projects going on at once. She dresses like she feels, and sometimes it looks like she is wearing five outfits at once (my sister and I often make fun of this). She can be sitting in a room full of her stuff (she pulls out every Monday), and when asked what is going on she says "This is organized chaos. It may look like a mess, but I know where everything is and where I am going with this madness."

Ministry is likened to organized chaos. Right now in my life I have 50 million things in the fire and as I sit and try to slowly allow things to settle before the next wave of tasks, I realize I am one of the people or piles on the Most High's agenda. I am on His to-do list and in order for the world to see Him in me, there is so much work that needs to be done. As I look from the outside in at His plan for my life it looks like chaos, but each step is ordered and He knows His intended outcome. Even when I think that I am caught in a whirlwind, I must trust that even it has purpose because of His providential care.

For instance, a tornado to many looks like junk spinning around destroying everyone's valuables and leaving people shattered and broken. A tornado has taken new meaning for me. A tornado is often times the only thing that can uproot comfortable and complacent people and allow them to rethink life choices. Now before you argue, think about it. People don't often move into a heavily tornado ridden area. More often than not, they are there because of generational ties and family history. The same with life struggles and trials. We do not just end up where we are, but we have often gotten comfortable and chose to merely set up shop and to endure the storms. We board up the windows of our heart preparing for the storms and repair the damage after the raging winds, instead of relocating and finding refuge in a safer climate. The wreckage becomes a part of who we are, our history, and we become the person who builds a tornado shelter. Just like the Israelites who did not want to leave Babylon (Jeremiah 51:45, Revelations 18:4) because of comfortability, many of us struggle to come out of her because her abominations have now become our traditions. We make trouble a part of our story and often get an adrenaline rush from the siren of danger and heartache. This is a mess.

This mess we are used to is the chaos that Yahuah did not necessarily orchestrate, but allows. It is allowed because of free will. It is allowed because many of us who know our heritage, know we are "show me" kind of people. We have to see things for ourselves and have to experience it to the fullest. But there is good news in calamity. This mess is not mess for His called and chosen, and that is the great joy and peace of Yah ordained calamity. The Bible says that all things work together for the good right?!... Well I submit that the statement is only partially right. The verse continues on with a clause for the application to your life, it says

And we know that all things work together for good to them that love YAH, to them who are the called according to his purpose.

Romans 8:28 (KJV)

For things to work out there is a stipulation applied to this promise. It says that you have to LOVE Yah, and you have to be called according to His purpose.

The issue with the mess, is that for some it can be just that. Mess! Self-created, self-appointed, self-anointed mess. This mess has no end and no ceasing, and if it does, it will not yield reward because Yah didn't ordain it. For the believer and the one called to GOOD WORKS (Ephesians 2:10), our mess is turned into testimony that is used in ministry. Our chaos is only chaos from the outside looking in. Our chaos is not chaos to the Master. The person with the idea in their head, like my mom and her five outfits at a time knows what plans she has for her ensemble. The same with Yah, He is our Father who loves us and He has the power to take mess (us and our lives) and use it for ministry. We are the clay and He is the potter.

As He sits at the wheel, He can change and modify what He wants the masterpiece to be. He may smash the clay at the wheel and apply pressure, it may seem like you are spinning out of control, but all the while you are in the midst of His wheel (will), and He is fashioning something out of you that seems good to Himself. It may look like a mess, but rest assured He is only preparing you for ministry! Yah is preparing us for a place where we can be trusted to minister about our hurt and our calamity and draw people to the one who brought us out of bondage! It is always to the Glory of HIS NAME!

DAY: TWENTY

Support Him

And let us not be weary in well doing: for in due season we shall reap, if we faint not.
Galatians 6:9

Wind and rain come and the tapestry may wear, but as long as the "ab" (ancient Hebrew for pole) is in place there is room for repair. Once the pole is removed, all who remain inside are vulnerable. The same is true for a fatherless home. If the condition of the so-called African American home is surveyed, you see a depressing picture of pole-less structures, leaving them exactly that, structureless.

The remedy for restoration of the family is restoring the strength of the family. As women, we are not the strength of the house in the sense that we hold it up. This is not our job. Although we have been forced into a role, and we have gotten comfortable, as we return to the path that our Heavenly Father has laid out, it is time to remove ourselves from the center of the proverbial tent of old, and place the man back at the center, as we do so we still have a role of strength, and the role is praising the man that takes the beating from the outside. We are to be his strength, as he is ours. We are to build him up, and teach our children to do the same. Make the man proud to weather the seasons and carry the heavy burden of holding the house together. He will gladly fight, hold, and defend a house where inside dwells his most prized possessions. He will stand strong knowing that under his care are his inheritance whom are depending, and relying on him with gladness. Today, put a smile on your faces, encourage the man who has taken the role as the priest of your home, and honor him in front of the world so he can stand with joy at his post.

Scripture Reading:

> *Again, if two lie together, then they have heat: but how can one be warm alone? And if one prevail against him, two shall withstand him; and a threefold cord is not quickly broken.*

Ecclesiastes 4:11-12 (KJV)

> *But if any provide not for his own, and specially for those of his own house, He hath denied the faith, and is worse than an infidel.*

I Timothy 5:8 (KJV)

> *Lo, children are an heritage of Yahuah: and the fruit of the womb is his reward. As arrows are in the hand of a mighty man; so are children of the youth. Happy is the man that hath his quiver full of them: they shall not be ashamed, but they shall speak with the enemies in the gate.*

Psalm 127:3-5 (KJV)

DAY: TWENTY-ONE

Keeping the Faith

Now faith is the substance of things hoped for, the evidence of things not seen.
Hebrews 11:1

Scripture tells us that the end is declared out of the beginning (Isa. 46:10). The reason this can be true for Yah and not so for us is because He does not change. While the world is constantly going through seasonal changes, while the government is going through policy changes, and while our lives are changing daily Yah is the constant One. Like a fortress in time of trouble, or an oasis in a dry land, He is always right where we need Him to be.

From the foundation of the world, YHWH has laid down a sure plan for His SEED, and their companions. In this promise is redemption and blessing that would extend to all generations. Like all scripture, as we work our way from the beginning toward the promise, we receive progressive revelation. Slowly but surely more of Yah's intricate plan is unveiled as reassurance to those whom stand firm in His way.

The word "keep" comes from the Hebrew word "shamar." This word means to protect, preserve, stay awake, guard, and to support. This is what our Heavenly Father wants us to do with His commandments. He wants us to support, protect, and preserve them, because in return, they are set up to do the same for us. Commandments and rules are meant to set healthy boundaries for the preservation of life. In our homes we set boundaries and laws that are age appropriate for each of our children. These laws are set up to allow them to grow, and to live long, healthy lives.

The scripture even co-signs our authority to do so by admonishing our children to obey us.

The same is true in scripture for our Heavenly Father. With Messiah as a witness to the necessity of obedience and keeping the commandments, we are to do so for the preservation of our lives, and those of our children. If we are obedient in all things to YHWH, even when we don't fully understand, as the children of the Living El, then it compels our children to obey to Him. Scripture teaches if we raise a child up in the way they should go, they will not depart from it (Proverbs 22:6). There is an owner manual to do, so and it is called the laws, precepts, and commandments of the Most High El.

Paul teaches in Galatians 3:24, that "Wherefore the law was our schoolmaster to bring us unto Christ, that we might be justified by faith." Faith is the graduation of the believer. Faith is the fruit of a child that is nurtured and raised properly. Once a seed is planted, and it takes roots and grows, it becomes securely fastened in the ground to bear more fruit. The laws of YHWH are the nutrients we need in order to become bearers of fruit. When we take a stand for righteousness, and are unwavering in our faith leaving any thing undone, it sets a precedence for the walk of our children. The Word is the seed and our children, if cultivated with diligence, will be the good soil whom will bear fruit for His Kingdom.

Scripture Reading:

Praise ye Yahuah. Blessed is the man that feareth Yahuah, that delighteth greatly in his commandments. His seed shall be mighty upon earth: the generation of the upright shall be blessed. Wealth and riches shall be in his house: and his righteousness endureth for ever.

Psalm 112:1-3 (KJV)

And I will put my spirit within you, and cause you to walk in my statutes, and ye shall keep my judgments, and do them.

Ezekiel 36:27 (KJV)

Blessed is the man that walketh not in the counsel of the ungodly, nor standeth in the way of sinners, nor sitteth in the seat of the scornful. But his delight is in the law of Yahuah; and in his law doth He meditate day and night. And He shall be like a tree planted by the rivers of water, that bringeth forth his fruit in his season; his leaf also shall not wither; and whatsoever He doeth shall prosper. The ungodly are not so: but are like the chaff which the wind driveth away. Therefore the ungodly shall not stand in the judgment, nor sinners in the congregation of the righteous. For Yahuah knoweth the way of the righteous: but the way of the ungodly shall perish.

Psalm 1 (KJV)

Bonus Studies

Cultivating Good Soil

But that on the good ground are they, which in an honest and good heart, having heard the word, keep it, and bring forth fruit with patience.
Luke 8:15

As a novice gardener and homesteader, I have been spending a lot of my time with my hands in the soil. My journey, like many others began with the conditions of food production. With the recent knowledge of GMOs, pesticides, and other harmful additives, getting back to what is pure has become very appealing. When I am out in the garden, especially with the children, questions are always posed. Recently my 4 year old asked who planted the other plants in the garden. My husband's response was that they were already in the soil. After hearing their dialogue I went into meditation about that thought. How can we possibly cultivate "good" soil, when it seems we are set up to fail before we even start?

What looked like good soil had something very fierce hiding beneath the surface. As long as the land was plowed, placed into nice little rows, but not yet watered, it looked like it didn't have any "defects." It was not until we started watering and waiting for those first sprouts that we saw differently. It seemed like almost overnight that the weed seeds had sprouted up. At first sight, it was as if the seeds we planted had quickly germinated. Not being entirely sure, we waited more days and added more water. Within a week, there were plants everywhere, but for some strange reason, they all looked the same. If it wasn't for knowing where we planted the good seed, we would not have had a clue of how to differentiate them from the weeds. The plants that came up in unified lines were potential good plants, while the ones that popped up all over were deemed weeds. Although we made daily assessments, we still were not sure. By the second week, there began to sprout plants that seemed to be right in line with the good plants. At this point, we were thoroughly confused. It was not until the third week that we were able to distinguish the weed plants from the ones that would yield crop. At this time, we were able to go through and pull up some of the weeds, but it seemed like the more we fed the good plants, the more the weeds grew.

This is a picture of the walk of the believer and often the process of cultivation we all go through. When the seed of truth is planted in our hearts, we immediately get excited about the process. We gleefully await the first harvest, but what we don't realize is that when we begin to water the seed of the Word, the weed seeds also will begin to sprout. The water often brings unwanted things to the surface. These are the weeds of our lives, the seeds that we have sown, and the seeds others have added to the soil of our hearts. While we don't like the annoyance of past offenses and hurts coming to the surface, this is the only way they can be identified and pulled up. If we neglect to water and till the soil because we fear the pain of weeding, then we will never experience the joy of the harvest.

Our job is to not get discouraged by the weeds. While they are there and often try to choke out or steal nutrients from our potential fruit, we must stay diligent to the process. The job of the adversary is to plant so many weeds that we grow discouraged, and throw the towel in, but Yeshua or Messiah told us the reward is to those who endure until the end. The reward is seeing the fruit of our perseverance. The reward are the lesson, and the stories we get to share that will encourage others during their periods of cultivation. These lessons will also be a testimony to us, because after harvest time, begins the next cultivation. For every season, there are different weeds. Through each season there is the process of identifying the weeds, and the Gardener's patience in order for the tender plant to grow. Yah is the gardener, and our hearts are where He is pruning and cultivating, so we can yield good fruit for the Kingdom. Sometimes the cultivation process is overwhelming, but not so to Yah. He is the kind and gentle Gardener who knows exactly when we are ripe for the picking. We must endure in His garden, so we can be counted in His harvest.

Scripture Reading:

> *And other fell on good ground, and did yield fruit that sprang up and increased; and brought forth, some thirty, and some sixty, and some an hundred.*

Mark 4:8 (KJV)

> *There is that scattereth, and yet increaseth; and there is that withholdeth more than is meet, but it tendeth to poverty. The liberal soul shall be made fat: and he that watereth shall be watered also himself.*

Proverbs 11:24-25 (KJV)

Read Matthew 13:1-58

Passing the Test

I know, my Elohim, that you test the heart and have pleasure in uprightness.
1 Chronicles 29:17

In Western thought, the whole world is viewed in a straight line. Everything that is old is behind us, and everything that is yet to come is in front of us. As we move "forward" in life, we believe we have progressed. Talk of age, birthdays, and milestones have us all convinced that even if we do nothing, we are going somewhere. This is furthest from the truth when it comes to our Heavenly Father. The teachings in scripture are all viewed in cycles, and by cycles, I mean circles. Yah doesn't pass people forward, He passes them higher, if they are obedient. Lots of people wonder why their lives seem stuck in a rut, and why they continue over and over again (you see it) to enter into the same trials and tribulations only to go through the process and be right back where they started. The reality is that they flunked with flying colors.

The reason why people encounter the same problems are because the problem mastered them and not vice versa. Trials are to prove us. Not to prove we can simply stand the storm, but to prove we can go through them in the way our Heavenly Father has outlined. He wants us to go through them, and come out better, not bitter. If we come out better, then we advance. If we come out bitter, it's back in the melting pot to remove the dross from the gold, and try again. As we go through our trials let us stand firm in His Word that we leave with a testimony and not an appointment for the same test.

Scripture Reading:

And thou, Solomon my son, know thou the Elohim of thy father, and serve him with a perfect heart and with a willing mind: for Yahuah searcheth all hearts, and understandeth all the imaginations of the thoughts: if thou seek him, He will be found of thee; but if thou forsake him, He will cast thee off for ever.

1 Chronicles 28:9

Lord, who shall abide in thy tabernacle? who shall dwell in thy holy hill? He that walketh uprightly, and worketh righteousness, and speaketh the truth in his heart. He that backbiteth not with his tongue, nor doeth evil to his neighbour, nor taketh up a reproach against his neighbour. In whose eyes a vile person is contemned; but Hehonoureth them that fear Yahuah. He that sweareth to his own hurt, and changeth not. He that putteth not out his money to usury, nor taketh reward against the innocent. He that doeth these things shall never be moved.

Psalm 15

Search me, O Yah, and know my heart: try me, and know my thoughts: And see if there be any wicked way in me, and lead me in the way everlasting.

Psalm 139:23-24

But as we were allowed of Yah to be put in trust with the gospel, even so we speak; not as pleasing men, but Yah, which trieth our hearts.

1 Thessalonians 2:4

I Yahuah search the heart, I try the reins, even to give every man according to his ways, and according to the fruit of his doings.

Jeremiah 17:10

Examine yourselves, whether ye be in the faith; prove your own selves. Know ye not your own selves, how that Yeshua HaMashiach is in you, except ye be reprobates?

2 Corinthians 13:5

Let us search and try our ways, and turn again to Yahuah.

Lamentations 3:40

About the Author

Huldah is a Messianic Hebrew descendant by way of Madagascar. It is the oral tradition of her family that they were taken from Madagascar on a Dutch slave ship to Holland. It was from Holland that her family made it to North Carolina. She was raised in a traditional Christian home as a Baptist, but through the learning of her heritage and her responsibility as a Child of the Living El, she has sought to learn the Hebrew language, and reclaim the culture and customs of her ancestors. Huldah is a college graduate. She has a passion for history and Yah's chosen people (blood born and grafted). Huldah works with the women and children of The Awakening Remnant Koalition in California. She is also co-owner of Royal Roots Natural Hair and Body Products.

"The real you is more interesting than the fake somebody else."

-Lauryn Hill

Inquiries or Questions should be addressed to:

The ARK
P.O. Box 3827
Pinedale, CA 93650

or emailed to:

AwakeningRemnant@gmail.com

Bibliography

Benner, Jeff. New Testament Greek To Hebrew Dictionary - 500 Greek Words
and Names Retranslated Back into Hebrew for English Reader. Virtualbook
worm.com, 2011. Print.

Benner, Jeff A. The Ancient Hebrew Lexicon of the Bible: Hebrew Letters, Words and
Roots Defined within Their Ancient Cultural Context. College Station, TX:
Virtualbookworm.com, 2005. Print.

Clark, Matityahu, and Samson Raphael Hirsch. Etymological Dictionary of Biblical Hebrew: Based on the Commentaries of Rabbi Samson Raphael Hirsch.
Jerusalem: Feldheim Pub., 1999. Print.

Scott, Bradford. "The WildBranch Ministry."The WildBranch Ministry. Web. 10 Nov.
2015.

Bibles

Biblia Hebraica Stutgartensia Septuagint

The Holy Bible, King James Version, Version 1769

Lexingham English Bible, Version 2012